Lost in the Store

T5-AFS-888

written by CLARE MISHICA
illustrated by JILL DUBIN

07 06 05 04 03 02 01 00   5 4 3 2 1

Library of Congress Card Number: 99-66968
ISBN 0-7847-1102-X

Standard
Publishing
Cincinnati, Ohio

"This is a big store," Mama said. "Stay close."

"We will," said Samantha. She whirled and twirled around with Bear. Bear went everywhere with Samantha.

Mama looked at dresses. She picked up a bright
red dress with a purple scarf. Samantha whirled and
twirled some more. She spun around the dress racks
until she was very dizzy.

"Oh, no," said Samantha, as she stopped spinning and sat down on the floor. "I think I left Bear in the garden department!"

Samantha looked over her shoulder.
Mama told me to stay close, but I'll only
be gone a minute, she thought. She hurried
back to the garden department.

There was Bear, right where she'd left him!

Samantha skipped back to the dresses with Bear.
"Here we are!" she giggled. But Mama wasn't there.

"Mama?" Samantha called. She ran down one aisle and up another, but she still did not see her mother.

"I think we're lost," she told Bear, and she gave
him a hug. "Don't worry. We'll find Mama."

Samantha saw someone wearing a yellow skirt. "Mama is wearing a yellow skirt," Samantha said to Bear. "Maybe that's Mama." Samantha and Bear hurried after the lady.

But the lady wearing the yellow skirt had gray curls and a flowery bag. "That's not Mama," said Samantha.

Samantha spotted someone wearing a hat with
red flowers. "That looks like Mama's hat," Samantha
told Bear. They ran down the aisle to look.

But the lady wearing the hat had a stroller and a baby. The baby waved at Samantha and Bear.

"That's not Mama," Samantha said and sighed. "Where could Mama be?"

Samantha's stomach felt like she'd swallowed a roller coaster. Hot tears slipped down Samantha's cheeks. They dripped on Bear and on the shiny floor. "Dear God," Samantha prayed. "I'm scared and I can't find my Mama."

Then Samantha remembered a song Mama had taught her. She sang to Bear,

"If you're lost in a store, what do you do?

Ask a friendly store clerk, and she'll help you.

March to the cash register—1, 2, 3.

Don't be afraid. Clerks can find your family."

"God helped me remember Mama's song,"
Samantha told Bear, "and now I know what to do!
I'll be brave and ask for help. Don't worry. You
won't have to talk." Samantha wiped her tears
and walked up to the front of the store.

"Hello," said Samantha in a wobbly voice to the clerk behind the cash register. "Can you help Bear and me find my mother?"

The clerk smiled and took her hand. "Sure I can," she said. "Let's go to the service desk. They'll make an announcement that everyone in the store will hear. What's your name?"

"Samantha Baker," said Samantha. "And this is Bear."

From the service desk, a big voice on the loudspeaker said, "Would Mrs. Baker please report to the service desk? Samantha is waiting for you. Mrs. Baker, please report to the service desk. Thank you."

Samantha smiled a little smile. "Now Mama will
know where to find us," she told Bear. Samantha
sat with Bear and waited.

Soon a happy voice said, "Samantha!" It was
Mama's voice. Samantha jumped off her chair
and into her mother's arms. She gave her mother
a giant hug, and her mother hugged her back.

"I'm so glad I found you," said Mama. "Why
didn't you stay with me?"

"I'm sorry," said Samantha. "Bear and I are going to stay very close to you now."

"That's good," said Mama. Then she gave Samantha and Bear another hug, and Samantha smiled the happiest and biggest smile of all.

Safety Suggestions for Parents

Help your child learn his full name, parents' names, and phone number.

Tell your child always to stay within hugging distance when you are out together in a public place.

Create a password for your child to use with people that you designate. For instance, you could give this password to someone who is going to pick your child up from school. That person would say the password to your child, and then she would know that it's safe to go with that person.

When you are out with your child in public, point out people and places your child could go to for help.

Teach your child that if he gets lost, he should stay where he can be seen. He should not look for *you*. You will find *him*.

Remind your child that God loves her and wants her to be safe!